VOLUME 1

Diese
Electrics
for
SCRAP

Ashley Butlin

The end for 08283 at Booth's yard, Rotherham, 25th November 1987. *Photo: Richard Lillie*

Acknowledgements

This book would not have been possible without the help and advice of many friends. Firstly, I must thank Nigel Trevena who initiated the preparation of the series. Also to David Pearce who helped to lay many of the ground work ideas.

For much of the factual information, I have drawn heavily on my own series of *Diesel Disposal* books which catalogue in detail the end of individual diesels, electrics and multiple units.

I am particularly indebted to the many photographers who have so readily given of their time and material, often at short notice. A special thank you must be extended to Vic Berry for allowing Paul Biggs and Richard Lillie access to his yard to take photographs for this project.

To all the British Rail employees who have helped, and especially the staff of BREL Public Relations Office, I record my gratitude. I must also thank my good friends of the RCTS and of the NREA and STARS railtours for their help both with information and photographs.

Finally, a very special thank you to my wife Jenny, who over the past months has become a mastermind with regard to withdrawn locomotives! Without her help, encouragement and words of advice, none of this would have been possible.

Ashley Butlin, September 1987

First published 1988

Designed by Nigel Trevena
Halftone photo reproduction by Oxford Litho Plates Ltd, Botley, Oxford
Printed by Century Litho, Penryn, Cornwall
Bound by Booth Bookbinders, Penryn, Cornwall

ISBN 0 906899 27 3

On 13th April 1983, 40056 emerges from New Mills tunnel en route for Booth's at Rotherham with 76008/28/09/01/36. *Photo: Gavin Morrison*

Published by
ATLANTIC TRANSPORT PUBLISHERS
Waterside House Falmouth Road
Penryn Cornwall TR10 8BE
England

Atlantic

Introduction

There is a morbid fascination in scrap yards. Silent, lifeless rows of locomotives, their paint faded and flaking, await the cutters torch, surrounded by signs of dereliction and decay; wheels, springs, body panels and broken glass, remnants of earlier machines that ended their days on the very same spot. Amongst the sidings, where the weed killer train never penetrates, sprout myriads of wild flowers. In early spring, the yellow coltsfoot readily grows between the ballast, to be followed in summer by tracts of purple rosebay willow-herb, that prolific weed of waste ground.

Grave yards for locomotives have existed as long as railways themselves, and be it Cohen's or Crewe, Draper's or Doncaster, enthusiasts have been drawn to them. Like mourners at a funeral, they come to pay their last respects.

It is now almost 20 years since the official end of steam on British Rail. A new generation

of rail enthusiasts is growing up. The story of the end of steam on BR has already been told in Atlantic's series *Steam for Scrap*. Now the diesels, electrics and multiple units that were built to replace steam are themselves being withdrawn, and this aspect of modern railway history is pictorially portrayed in *Diesels for Scrap*. In this first volume, we shall take an overall view of the subject; from 1940 to 1986, from storage to disposal, from private yards to BREL. Over the years the story unfolds as both locomotives and units are withdrawn from service and come to the end of their working days.

Although diesels and electrics have been operating in this country since before the turn of the century, it was not until the Modernisation Plan of 1955 was announced that a major building programme was initiated and diesels and electrics began to appear in large numbers. In addition to the diesel shunters already ordered or under construction, this plan called for 174 mainline diesels of 13 classes to be built and evaluated over a period of several

years. From the lessons learnt from these pilot scheme designs, BR planned to place further orders for the production classes. However, by 1958, the financial situation of the railways was causing serious concern. Following government pressure, the BTC undertook a reappraisal of the Modernisation Plan and recommended its acceleration. It projected a total fleet of 2,300 mainline diesels to be in operation by the end of 1963, so hastening the end of steam on BR. Such a move inevitably meant that the pilot scheme evaluation plan had to be abandoned even before some classes had been introduced into service. Orders were placed for many more locomotives of types, the true potential of which was largely unknown. It was these decisions that were to have repercussions for many years to come, as designs were delivered that did not meet the expectations originally set for them.

By 1963, significant changes to the railway traffic patterns meant that a further reappraisal of the locomotive fleet was called for. Studies showed that there was an imbalance of motive power, with a preponderance of locomotives in the 1000/1250hp range but an acute shortage of the 2000/2500hp types. Studies also looked at the availability and maintenance costs of each class. These showed that some classes fell significantly below others in both reliability/availability and maintenance costs. Specifically, diesel-hydraulics were shown to be as reliable as diesel-electrics but at a much higher maintenance rate, and their future was immediately brought into question. Inter-regional transfers took place in an attempt to even out the power imbalance problem. A number of small non-standard classes were withdrawn, reducing both the number of different classes with which drivers needed to be conversant, and the number of spares which needed to be carried. Standardisation was becoming the order of the day.

Further interim reports in 1966 and 1967 resulted in the very efficient but low powered Class 20s being run together in pairs so as to produce a 2000+hp combination and avoid the need for brake tenders on unfitted freights. By 1970, the end of the hydraulics seemed inevitable. Further transfers provided the Western Region with motive power sufficient for all but the Westerns to be eventually withdrawn.

ABOVE: 55 tons of scrap metal — all that remains of former LMSR diesel shunter 12012 at Bolton MPD on the 7th August 1968, cut by local scrap dealer W. Hatton. Behind, an unidentified Class 5 awaits the same fate. *Photo: H.L. Holland*

RIGHT: Whilst one was used to seeing convoys of withdrawn steam locomotives heading for scrapping at one of the many scrap merchants in South Wales, the sight of withdrawn diesels being so transported was far less common. In this view, Warship D800 *Sir Brian Robertson* (the doyen of the class), North British Class 22 D6314, and Warship D863 *Warrior* are seen passing Gloucester North hauled by Class 47 D1680 (later 47094) on 13th July 1969. All three were en route to Cashmore's at Newport. They entered that yard the following week and within three days of arrival, D800 had been completely cut. These were the only Class 42/43 'Warships' not cut at Swindon Works. *Photo: Norman Preedy*

While all these changes were taking place effecting main line classes, a reduction in the number of freight centres resulted in almost a halving of the shunter fleet by 1970, from 2000 to just over 1000 locomotives. Withdrawals were again concentrated on older classes and those which were non-standard. What remained in service were, with a few specialised exceptions, classes 03, 08, & 09.

Three significant factors in the late seventies were to have far reaching effects on BR's withdrawal policy. These were: the introduction to traffic of the High Speed Trains, the introduction of purpose built freight loco-motives, and the economic recession at the time. The introduction of the HSTs allowed a cascading downwards of the previous main-line locomotives to lesser routes and roles, and the withdrawal of older machines. At the same time, BR introduced their new freight locomotives, the Class 56, to be followed later by the Class 58s. Once again, these allowed movement of stock and ultimately the withdrawal of many locomotives.

When the recession began to hit BR's freight traffic in 1980, many locomotives were mothballed, officially with a view to putting them back into traffic at a later date, but with few exceptions this mothballing meant with-drawal.

As a result of these three factors, by 1981, inroads were being made into classes 08, 25, 40, 46 & 55, whilst several classes were already extinct, notably the 24s. As will be seen in chapter 6, during the eighties further changes to the locomotive fleet are taking place constantly.

This then is the story of the rise and fall of the diesels and electrics; a constantly changing scene as new practice and technology renders the old obsolete and condemns it to the scrap yard.

ABOVE: Six Deltics have avoided the cutter's torch and passed into preservation. Included amongst them is 55019 *Royal Highland Fusilier* which went to the North Yorkshire Moors Railway in August 1982. Previous to this, it was stored at Doncaster for eight months, where it was photographed surrounded by rosebay willow-herb, that ever present weed of waste ground. At the time of writing, 55019 is at the Midland Railway Centre at Butterley. *Photo: Brian Morrison*

LEFT: 03175 was cut at Doncaster in November 1983, although the cab, as seen here, has remained in the scrap yard ever since, in use as a bothy, a definite necessity in the winter months. *Photo: R.S.M. Brown*

Reasons for withdrawal

Withdrawing a locomotive from service is a decision which cannot be undertaken lightly. New engines do not come cheap and although a Class 47 may have cost £100,000 back in the sixties, a replacement Class 58 or HST would today cost BR almost ten times as much. Consequently, great thought has to go into withdrawal decisions and all other options need to be considered. Economics is a major concern of railway operators.

Life expired

Regular and reliable servicing is a feature of BR, even though the commuter arriving 20 minutes late due to "engine failure at Strawberry Hill" may well not agree. Even with the best servicing possible, all machinery is prone to the onset of old age, and when this is the case, servicing becomes more expensive as an increasing number of components require replacing. There inevitably comes the time when repairs are no longer economically viable and it is cheaper to withdraw the locomotive concerned; life expired. It is usual, in these cases, to salvage as many reusable components as possible which can be used to help keep the remainder of the class operational. In fact, locomotives may well be withdrawn for that very purpose; having supplied many essential parts for months previous, withdrawal of what remains is the only option available. It is not just small parts or even power units and bogies that are reused. Complete cabs can be transplanted to keep accident damage victims in service.

Accident and fire victims

A visit to any BREL workshop will produce a number of engines in for repair. Most are minor shunting victims, but a far more serious accident occasionally takes place. When major damage has occurred, then once again economics become an essential consideration. Is repair an option? If it is a class that is already being withdrawn through old age, then even minor damage can result in withdrawal, but if it is a new locomotive with lengthy life expectancy, repairs usually follow. Over the years there have been exceptions to this. When less than a year old, Class 37 D6983 was involved in a serious accident when it collided with equally new Class 47 D1671 *Thor* at Bridgend. Both locomotives were extensively damaged and subsequently withdrawn. They were cut by local scrap dealer, R.S. Hayes of Bridgend.

In a similar manner, fire damage victims may or may not be repaired depending on circumstances. Many of the early withdrawals of Classes 26 & 27 were as a result of fire damage.

Surplus to operating requirements

In the late sixties, changes in operating procedures resulted in many small uneconomical yards being closed and, simultaneously, better utilisation of available motive power. As a result, BR had a surplus of locomotives on its books. Large scale withdrawals followed; many of the small non-standard shunter classes were withdrawn and the total shunter fleet was reduced from around 2000 to just over 1200. Only a few of the withdrawals were old and life expired; the vast majority were in fact only a few years old and hardly run-in. Many of these found further use with Industrial concerns, some still giving invaluable service today, almost 20 years after being sold.

Non-standard

It was not just shunters that were surplus to requirements. Mainline classes of the lower power range were also withdrawn; those non-standard with the remainder of the fleet and, in most cases, the less successful of the pilot scheme classes. Had the general public been fully aware of the situation at the time, both BR and the government could have found themselves with awkward questions to answer. Not only were almost new diesels involved, but Class 82 & 83 electrics. Built only a few years earlier for the WCML, they were proving so unreliable that BR considered scrapping large numbers. In the event, following storage at Bury for a number of years, they were refurbished at Doncaster Works and gave good service through to the early eighties.

LEFT: Old age finally caught up with the English Electric built Class 40s. Withdrawals through the eighties were steady and in 1985 only the pioneer D200 (40122) remained in active passenger service. This dramatic view of 40069 at Doncaster Works on 10th October 1984 clearly shows the great size and bulk of these machines. *Photo: Gavin Morrison*

RIGHT: On 31st July 1967, English Electric DP2 was involved in a serious accident south of Thirsk while hauling the 12.00 London to Edinburgh express. With his speedometer reading 80mph, the driver spotted derailed wagons of a Cliffe-Uddingston cement train littering the track. In spite of an emergency brake application, DP2 collided with the wagons and was derailed. DP2 was removed to York TMD, where it was photographed in August. Being both non-standard and a prototype, its withdrawal was inevitable. On the 8th September 1967, DP2 was hauled back to Vulcan Foundry and cut early the following year. Its diesel engine was reconditioned and used in D400 (later 50050). Ironically, the Class 50s were ordered by British Rail as a result of the success of DP2, and were being constructed by English Electric at the time of the latter's untimely demise.
Photo: P.B. Whitehouse (Millbrook House Collection)

Reasons for withdrawal

LEFT: Built by English Electric at Vulcan Foundry during 1959, the 'Baby Deltic' pilot scheme class was never a great success, in spite of various attempts by English Electric to improve reliability. In the era of mass withdrawals in the late sixties/early seventies, the class fell victim on the grounds of being non-standard. All, except D5901 and D5908, finally found their way to George Cohen's Kettering yard where in September 1973 demolition of D5909 was well under way. The power unit had been removed, and only the cabs and bogies remained to be cut. *Photo: P. Butler*

LEFT: Over the years, the Class 27s have become notorious for their pyrotechnic antics in Scotland. Many of the early withdrawals were as a result of fire. The damage caused to 27044, photographed at Eastfield on 5th September 1980, is all too clear and typical of what a fire will do to an engine once it gets a hold.
Photo: Gavin Morrison

BELOW: Bolton TMD, 16th July 1968, and four Drewry Class 04 shunters surplus to requirement: D2227, D2234, D2224 & D2226, all withdrawn three months earlier on 13th April, await a tow to Albert Draper's yard at Hull. Movement came in September, with numbers 24, 26 & 27 being cut the following month. D2234 remained intact at Draper's until May of the following year. In comparison to the hundreds of steam locomotives which were sold to Draper's, these were just four of the seven diesels the firm purchased.

Proof that withdrawal for the majority of this class was premature lies in the fact that many other withdrawn 04s escaped cutting and passed into industrial use where, even today, they are still giving excellent service.
Photo: J. Corkill

Locos in store

Prior to official withdrawal, locomotives are often found in store for varying lengths of time pending an official condemnation notice being issued. This is particularly the case for accident or fire damage victims, or a failure of a member of a declining class where a fixed cost limit determines whether a locomotive can be repaired and returned to service. Once estimates are available, a decision quickly follows.

The time span of storage preceding withdrawal varies. Often it is only a matter of days or weeks, but for others it is much longer and could well depend on the nature of the repair required in relation to the future policies regarding that class. Although possibly not economically viable for individual repair, where two members of the same class are involved, they may well be combined to produce one good locomotive. The record for storage rests with the former NER electric locomotive No13, later 26600, which was stored for almost 30 years mostly at Darlington Works before finally being condemned and sold to a Sheffield scrap merchant.

While in store, cannibalising of spare parts to keep other members of the class in service is a regular occurrence and this invariably seals the fate of a loco. Locos are even moved from one depot to another to provide a source of spares.

Once officially withdrawn, locomotives must remain in store until final disposal can be arranged. Although this is usually on the depot where withdrawal took place, limited space can mean that locomotives need to be moved either to another depot or to yards where lack of space is not a problem.

Over the past 20 years, there have been a number of occasions when long rows of stored locos have accumulated within yards. The mass withdrawal of 51 diesel-hydraulics, including 29 Warships, at the end of the summer timetable in October 1971, followed by an equal number in January 1972, inevitably caused storage problems at Western Region depots. This resulted in several dumps forming on the region, notably Bristol Marsh Junction where upwards of 40 locos could be found awaiting onward movement to Swindon Works for cutting. Later in the seventies, the withdrawal of over 100 Class 24s in one year found equally lengthy rows of redundant engines in Basford Hall Sidings, Crewe, and Kingmoor Yard, Carlisle.

Finally, robbed of many parts, vandalised, with paint fading and no longer serviceable, the loco's last journey takes place. Cannibalised locos need to be made safe for this journey and, to minimise problems, dead engine movements are limited both in size and speed. Special permission has to be granted for exceptional movements such as the 14 Class 82/83 electrics which were towed from Stoke on Trent to Leicester on 26th September 1984, destined for Vic Berry's yard. Despite precautions, journeys may not always go according to plan. Following protracted storage, hot boxes readily occur and journeys may well be terminated short of their final destinations. Engines are found shunted into the most unexpected sidings and yards awaiting rectification of problems to allow completion of the journey. Recently, to avoid some of

these problems, Berry's of Leicester have part-cut locos at depots and then transported the cut sections by road to their Leicester yard for final cutting.

LEFT, TOP: On the mass withdrawal of the diesel-hydraulics during 1971-72, St Phillips Marsh, Bristol, became a temporary home to large numbers of diesel-hydraulics and upwards of 40 locomotives could be found awaiting forward movement to Swindon for scrapping. Here, D818, D6322, D6323, D6315, D868, D819, D822, D808, D843, D833, D855 and D857 all await their final journey on 3rd November 1971, the day on which all except D6323/15 and D843 were withdrawn. *Photo: Norman Preedy*

LEFT, BOTTOM: At Newton Abbot on 19th

July 1972, Warships D827/66/11 have a further two months to wait before it is their turn to be towed to Swindon Works. *Photo: G.F. Gillham*

ABOVE: The Class 52 Westerns were, of course, the last of the hydraulics to be withdrawn from service. As with other classes at the end of their careers, many were cannibalised to keep others in service. This work was usually undertaken at Laira, the home depot of the class in its final years. On 15th September 1973, seven of the class: D1004/17/38/39/42/32/20 await onward movement to Swindon. At this time not all were officially withdrawn, but broken or missing windows in D1004 show that their days are numbered. *Norman Preedy*

Locos in store

LEFT, TOP: Hull Dairycoates shed in June 1968, and recently withdrawn Class 14s await disposal. They were built at Swindon in 1964-65 but the work for which they were designed, namely pick-up freight, had all but ceased before the first of the class entered service. Initially, all were allocated to the Western Region, but by December 1966 a batch had been transferred to Humberside where, unfortunately, the very same situation existed. Withdrawals followed in April 1968, with 46 of the class being sold into industrial service at bargain prices. *Photo: Tim Edmonds*

LEFT, BOTTOM: Of all the classes stored, the Claytons must hold the record for the number of times individual members were moved around Scotland from location to location. The Scottish Region seemed very reluctant to dispose of locomotives that had been built to become BR's principal 1000hp Class. On 15th November 1973, D8573, D8613, D8548 and D8504 all wait at Polmadie. These were a few of the class which had spent almost 12 months during 1972 stored at Ardrossan on the Ayrshire coast. It was August 1975 before D8573 & D8613 were sold to McWilliam's at Shettleston, and the other two made the long journey south to Cashmore's at Great Bridge. *Photo: Brian Morrison*

RIGHT, TOP: During the eighties, the North Yard at Swindon Works became a storage site for numerous withdrawn locomotives awaiting cutting. The yard is partially visible from the Gloucester line, but with rows of locomotives present, only a few could ever be seen from a passing train, and even for most visits the yard was not included in the itinerary. In this rare view of the yard, 21st September 1985, only a few of the 125 locomotives present in the yard are visible. Most are 08s and 25s with a few dmus waiting forwarding to Mayer Newman's at Snailwell. *Photo: Richard Lillie*

RIGHT, BOTTOM: Towards the end of 1987, withdrawn stock began to accumulate at March TMD where a high security profile was placed on the locomotives to prevent vandalism. During 1988, March TMD is being made responsible for component recovery from withdrawn stock prior to it being sold for scrap. On a grey morning, 13th December 1987, forty one locos from Class 03, 08, 20, 25, 45 & 47 were present at the depot. *Photo: Richard Lillie*

The early years

For more than 80 years, diesel and electric locomotives have been at work in the British Isles. To most enthusiasts in the steam era, diesels and electrics were looked on very much as boxes on wheels, and limited film supplies were rarely wasted on them. Consequently, some of the following photographs are extremely rare.

By 1920, the NER was running a fleet of 10 electric locomotives between Shildon and Newport, Co. Durham, hauling heavy coal trains. Sir Vincent Raven, Chief Mechanical Engineer of the NER, had ambitious plans to electrify the East Coast line from Newcastle to York. He had the first passenger electric loco ready for service, but his plans were thwarted by the 1923 amalgamation, the newly formed LNER not taking up his ideas. Sadly, even the Shildon-Newport scheme ran into difficulties during the recession of the thirties with falling traffic due to the decline in coal traffic. In addition, the overhead line equipment was becoming life expired. All the electrics were laid up in store at Darlington until BR days when they passed to Wanty's at Sheffield for scrap.

Other regions were experimenting in diesel power, with varying degrees of success. The LMS achieved most success with its diesel shunters. Experimentation began in the 1930s with the construction of 11 assorted designs, and although not all lived up to expectation, sufficient expertise was obtained to encourage the placing of further orders. Twenty 0-6-0 shunters entered service at Willesden, Crewe and Kingmoor during 1936. All but three of this initial order were to see military service during World War 2. Further orders were placed during 1938 and 1940, the locos being built at Derby. Again, many of these were loaned to the War Department and failed to return from war duties. By Nationalisation in 1948, the LMSR had over 40 shunters on their books, and it was to be from experience gained principally from these that the ubiquitous 08s were developed in the early fifties.

Other regions also dabbled with diesel shunters. All had small fleets of diesel and petrol fired vehicles which were in use with engineers departments, many having been built in the twenties. In 1935, the GWR had ordered a single 0-6-0 shunter from R&W Hawthorn Leslie and Co. of Newcastle, while two years later, the SR had built three 0-6-0s of their own at Ashford works. It was to be 1944 before the LNER entered into diesel experiments with four 0-6-0s built at their own Doncaster Works.

Whilst the LMS had had the success with shunters, the GWR developed diesel railcars. By 1942 they had a fleet of 38 which were later to influence BR to build diesel multiple units in 1954, the first Derby Lightweight, the predecessors of an enormous fleet of units constructed mainly between 1956 and 1960.

On the mainline diesel front, at nationalisation BR inherited only one example, LMS built 10000, with its companion 10001 almost completed at Derby. The SR contributed two electric locos, Bulleid designed 20001 and 20002, while from the Eastern Region came 14 electrics. These composed the 11 that had been in store, plus two dating back to 1904 working on the quayside at Newcastle and the prototype Class 76 26000, *Tommy* which at the time was still on loan to Netherlands Railway.

Against this assorted background of diesel and electric development, BR began to formulate its own modernisation plans. Had it not been for a shortage of diesel fuel at the end of the war and lack of funds, diesel and electric power may have arrived sooner rather than later. While British railways had received considerable damage during the war, it was not as substantial as on the continent where the railways required more extensive rebuilding, hence electrification in Europe took place much sooner than here. In the event, the newly formed British Railways embarked on an ambitious building programme of steam locomotives. This, with hindsight, was not to be the best move. Much money was wasted on steam locomotives which were only to see a few years' service.

Prior to the Second World War, car ownership was very limited, but in the fifties this was to change. No longer were the railways the only means of getting from A to B. The family car would often cover the journey in half the time. And, even as the 1955 Modernisation Plan was being announced and implemented, other factors were coming to bear that greatly affected the railways. The 1955 Modernisation Plan dealt the final death blow to steam. The story of how BR scrapped 16,000 steam locomotives between 1958 and 1968 has already been told in Atlantic's *Steam for Scrap* series.

LEFT: Built at Derby Works in 1932 on the frames and running gear of MR 1821, originally an O-6-OT built at Vulcan Foundry in 1891, the 'new' 1831 became the first LMS diesel hydraulic shunter constructed to ascertain the feasibility of diesel traction. On entering service in the Derby area, 1831 was not found to be a great success and by November 1936 it had been placed in store, being officially withdrawn in September 1939. The outbreak of war and the need for electrical generators meant that 1831 was not disposed of but converted at Crewe Works to a mobile electric power unit, MPU3. It spent the war years in the Coventry area, but was later noted out of use at Crewe South MPD. By August 1949 it had moved to Crewe Works where it is seen devoid of identification, and coupling rods. It was to be a further two years before it was finally cut for scrap. *Photo: F. Hornby*

ABOVE: Surely the most famous diesel of them all, 10000 was Britain's first main line diesel locomotive. Constructed at Derby Locomotive Works, it entered service one month before Nationalisation, to be followed in the following July by its partner, 10001. This pair, along with 10201-03, were to pioneer diesel traction in Britain throughout the fifties and influence future Derby designs, notably the Peaks.

By December 1962, 10000 was in store at Derby Works along with the Southern Region trio of 10201-3. For over five years these four remained at Derby awaiting a final decision as to their future. Finally, on the 9th February 1968, all were moved to Cashmore's yard at Great Bridge, where 10000 is seen through a haze of smoke generated by the cutters' torches and framed by the remains of some of the steam engines it had helped to oust from service.
Photo: Tom Middlemas

LEFT: When tenders were issued for construction of the 3000 plus dmus in the mid fifties, Cravens Ltd of Sheffield received orders for 405 units. The last 100 power cars supplied by Cravens to this order differed from earlier examples in having a single Rolls-Royce engine and hydraulic transmission. In service, this batch was to give considerable problems, not the least of which was a tendency to catch fire. For the passengers, serious vibration problems made them a noisy class in which to travel. All in all, they were not a great success, and these faults and their non standard nature made them early candidates for withdrawal once sufficient cascaded vehicles were made available, by line closure, to replace them. By 1969, many were in store, awaiting disposal, at Rugby, where all reusable components including doors and seats were removed before the bodies were sold off privately to King's at Norwich or Wards, Briton Ferry. On 15th February 1969, M51723 from Cricklewood, heads a line of units outside the former electric depot at Rugby. Note the variations in livery: 51723 has small yellow warning panels, while the second unit has a full yellow front and units three and four both retain their original green livery and lining. *Photo: H.L. Holland*

The early years

RIGHT: Wanty's scrap yard at Catcliffe, Rotherham, in the spring of 1951, and former NER electric 26505 rests amongst the piles of scrap. Built at Darlington in 1914 for use on heavy freight trains on the Newport-Shildon line in County Durham, this pioneer class of electrics was to remain in service until January 1935 when a decline in coal traffic meant they were placed in store. Only one was ever to work again, namely 26510 which was rebuilt at Doncaster during 1942 for use as depot shunter at the newly opened Ilford car sheds. With the exception of 26510 cut at Doncaster and 26504 cut at Darlington, the remainder joined 26505 at Wanty's.
Photo: B. Hinchliffe

ABOVE: Some of the earliest diesels to end their days at Swindon were the Simplex diesels built in the twenties for use by the Engineer's Departments. No.26, at Swindon on 12th December 1956, was the last to be built, in 1927, and spent its working life at Didcot Provender Stores until put to store at Swindon in the mid fifties. It was to be the end of 1960 before this diminutive machine was reduced to a very small pile of scrap.
Photo: F. Hornby

LEFT: It was the GWR which pioneered diesel railcars with its AEC units built in the thirties. These proved to be a remarkable success and passengers increased to such an extent on some of their services that the cars had to be replaced by steam hauled trains of two or three coaches. As more modern units came into service, so the older AEC units were withdrawn. By October 1962, all had been condemned. Nearly two years later in June 1964, W21W remains at Swindon depot sidings, its windows smashed and its bodyside carrying the handpainted "COND" sign which appeared on so many vehicles at this time.
Photo: D.J. Everson

TOP: It is an often overlooked fact that London Underground was, for many years, the most extensive electric system in the country. Although the vast majority of the fleet were multiple units, in 1904 and 1906, two batches, each consisting of ten Bo-Bo electric locomotives were built for outer suburban work. These were not a great success and were rebuilt by Metropolitan-Vickers in 1922. After rebuilding, they became a common sight hauling Aylesbury trains between the City, Baker Street and Rickmansworth. Most were taken out of traffic in January 1962, although six remained in service for a further two months. Of these, Nos. 2, 7, 16 & 18 were stored at Mitre Bridge where they were photographed on 28th March 1962. Three years later they were moved to Rugby, being finally cut in July 1966.
Photo: Tom Middlemas

BOTTOM: During the Second World War, many LMS diesel shunters were loaned to the WD and sent overseas. Not all returned to this country; some were destroyed in action, captured by the enemy or sold to various countries after the war. The WD also had a number of their own shunters, supplied direct. 70249 was one such locomotive, and was photographed in a derelict state at Suez in 1944/45.
Photo: R.G. Jarvis (Millbrook House Collection)

The early years

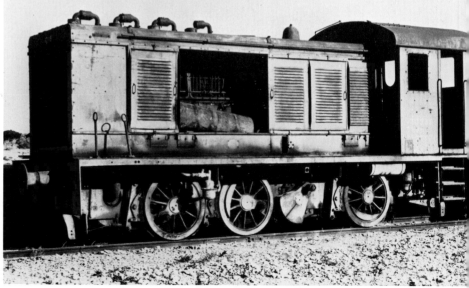

The role of the private yards

When BR sold four Churchward Moguls 5312, 5360, 5392 & 5396 to Woodham Brothers at Barry in March 1959, it started a process which snowballed through the sixties, as thousands of redundant steam engines were sold off to private scrapyards. As the supplies of steam engines came to an end in 1967-68, some yards looked for new sources of material to cut. Many ceased to deal in railway supplies completely, whilst others turned to coaches and wagons. Only a few established yards turned their hands to cutting the new motive power. In addition, several new companies began to trade in redundant diesels; notably C.F. Booth Ltd of Rotherham who were to handle numerous diesels. The numbers were comparatively small: although British Rail was withdrawing both shunters and mainline classes that were considered non-standard or surplus to requirement, total sales of diesels in the four years between 1967-70 failed to exceed total sales of steam locomotives for just four months during the peak scrapping years of 1964-66. Many shunters, in perfect working order, were bought by industrial concerns at scrap prices for re-use.

Only a very limited number of yards were to purchase diesels in any numbers. Even yards like Cohen's, Booth's and Slag Reduction, major concerns in terms of numbers of locos processed, were to scrap less than one hundred locos apiece, whilst most private yards could count their total numbers processed on the fingers of their hands. Later, in the seventies, when mass withdrawals of mainline classes took place, virtually all scrapping was taken over by BREL and the private yards came to a virtual end. Not until 1986-87 when reorganisation of BREL resulted in a cessation of cutting at Swindon, Doncaster and Glasgow did sales in any significant numbers to private yards once again take place. Now, though, changes in the law relating to asbestos removal meant that only firms with the specialised facilities needed for handling this deadly material were allowed to tender for locomotives. Consequently, Vic Berry's at Leicester has become the major outlet for withdrawn locos.

In terms of total scrappings, the private yards have only played a minor (but nevertheless fascinating) role. Because so few yards took part, and because most dealt with so few locomotives, photographs from some yards are extremely rare and, maybe, even non-existent. We are indebted to those photographers, many of them die-hard steam enthusiasts, who took the time, trouble and effort to record the diesels they saw awaiting scrapping in these small yards around the country.

ABOVE: Cohen's of Kettering took their first steam engines for scrapping in the spring of 1964. These first few came from the Southern Region and their appearance on the Midland caused great excitement amongst enthusiasts. Just as rare was the movement northwards to Kettering of London Transport Tube stock which also ended its days at Cohen's. These two views show (top) Piccadilly Line stock at Cohen's in the final stages of cutting on 1st April 1964, while (below), a month later, further vehicles had arrived and were awaiting their turn, surrounded by the cut remains of previous stock. *Photo: (top) Robin Leleux, (below) Les Wade via John Stretton*

The role of the private yards

RIGHT: Only a few diesel shunters ended their days at Bird's, Long Marston, but of those that did, most were processed very slowly, several remaining in the yard for many years. In theory, some were serviceable, but parked off the rails, this status must be questionable. In comparison, Class 03 D2190 was cut some 14 months after arriving at the yard. It was photographed on 28th July 1970, and cut a few weeks later. *Photo: Norman Preedy*

BELOW: Metropolitan-Cammell has had a long association with BR, being the first private contractor to be awarded a contract in 1955 to build diesel multiple units. These first lightweight twin units were allocated to East Anglia and the LMR Bury-Bacup service. In appearance they were unmistakeably Metropolitan-Cammell and, on the whole, a success. Unfortunately, their Yellow Diamond coupling code became non-standard as newer units were built, making them incompatible with other vehicles. As services in East Anglia were withdrawn, so were the units. By the late sixties, many

were in store at the former Ipswich MPD awaiting disposal. Some went to Bird's at Long Marston where an unidentified example is seen in October 1978, almost 10 years after the class was withdrawn from service. *Photo: Graham Scott-Lowe*

ABOVE: Despite its comprehensive electric system, the Southern has never run an extensive fleet of electric locomotives. After the three Co-Cos, 20001-3, built in 1941-48, the 24 Class 71s built for the Kent Coast lines in 1958 were the only straight electrics on the Southern. The more successful Class 73 electro-diesels, with their dual power systems, were much preferred. As a result, in the mid-sixties, when several of the Class 71s were considered surplus to requirement, they were converted to electro-diesels, the Class 74s. Unlike the 73s with their EE diesels, the 74s were fitted with Paxman diesels, and these did not prove anywhere near as reliable. Although they were to give 10 years service, they were withdrawn in 1977 on the grounds of being non-standard. Unusually for this time, the class, with the exception of 74010, were sold off privately. Five ended their days at Bird's, Long Marston, where only an unidentified cab of one of the locomotives remained on 21st October 1978. *Photo: Graham Scott-Lowe*

RIGHT: Draper's at Hull handled many steam locomotives during the sixties but only a handful of diesels passed through the yard. Amongst these was a single Class 17, D8605 from Thornaby. It arrived at Hull in May 1969, six months after being withdrawn, and remained intact in the yard for just over a year before being cut in June 1970. It had seen exactly four years' service before withdrawal. *Photo: Tim Edmonds*

LEFT: Flanked by two steam locomotives, 15202 stands in the sidings outside Cashmore's yard at Newport in October 1966, almost two years after it had been withdrawn from Ashford. This was one of a batch of three early shunters built by the Southern Region, with English Electric engines, at their Ashford Works in 1937.
Photo: D.J. Everson

BELOW: The North Tyneside loop line from Newcastle Central Station to Tynemouth via Jesmond and Wallsend has the distinction of being electrified twice; firstly in 1904 by the NER in an attempt to win back much lost custom when trams began working in the streets of Newcastle; secondly, in 1982, when the north loop of the Metro was completed. In June 1967 the lines were de-electrified and the services worked by DMUs until 1982.

In 1937, the LNER took delivery of 64 articulated twin units built by Metropolitan Cammell, and these units served the lines until cessation of the initial electric services. After the last train had run on 17th June 1967, the cars were sold for scrap, trailer open second E29238E ending its days at local scrap dealers, Hughes Bolckow of Blyth where it was noted on 13th July 1967. Through the broken windows can be viewed the bucket seats, a feature of these units.
Photo: I.S. Carr

The role of the private yards

RIGHT: Withdrawn from Polmadie in October 1971, Class 17 D8525 was initially stored for 12 months at its home depot prior to a further three years at Glasgow Works. Surprisingly, unlike many others of the class, it was not cut by BREL at Glasgow but sold along with ten others in September 1975 to Archie King of Norwich. February 1976 finds dismantling well under way within King's yard. With the exception of these Claytons, King's only cut four other diesels, Class 04s D2210 and D2240, and former LNER built 15000 and 15002.
Photo: David Pearce

LEFT: Motherwell Machinery and Scrap Company Ltd of Wishaw, Motherwell, was one of the major yards dealing in scrap steam locomotives, several hundred passing through the yard in the mid-sixties. In comparison, the firm only purchased four diesel shunters: Hunslet Class 05 D2577, North British D2725 & D2753 in September 1967 and Class 05 D2576 in August 1968. All four locomotives had been withdrawn by BR as surplus to requirement following implementation of the National Traction Plan. D2725 was photographed awaiting scrapping at the yard in the autumn of 1967.
Photo: Keith Romig

The role of the private yards

Kettering, a small market town on the Midland main line, may have for ever remained as an obscure station announced between "Wellingborough and Market Harborough" had it not been for George Cohen's yard. Situated on the site of the former Cransley Ironstone furnaces about one mile west of Kettering station, the actual yard could not be seen from the main line. However, from 1964-74, withdrawn loco-motives were often to be seen in the sidings at Kettering awaiting a final move to Cohen's. The yard itself was clearly visible from the main A43 Kettering-Northampton road, and from a convenient farm track that ran alongside the full length of the yard.

These two photographs show typical views of Cohen's during the diesel years. (A full feature on the yard is planned for Volume 2.)

ABOVE: 1st March 1969 and cutting of Class 10 D3441 is well advanced while work has still to commence on fellow class member D3477.

BELOW: The excellent external condition of Class 15s D8236/40/35 hides the fact that all three will never run again. Over half the class were withdrawn in 1968, the majority going to Cohen's. The remainder of the class survived until 1971 when they were withdrawn and, after storage at Ipswich, sent to Crewe Works for cutting.
Photos: H.L. Holland

C.F. Booth's scrap yard at Rotherham only commenced handling locomotives after the end of steam. From 1967-71 many diesel shunters passed through the yard, and in 1983 many of the withdrawn Class 76s ended their days at Booth's. Between times, very few locomotives entered the yard, although withdrawn units were common.

LEFT: On 7th May 1968, the demolition of newly arrived shunters D2951 and D2609, from Goole, had already commenced. Numerous shunters passed through Booth's yard during the peak years of 1968-69. Most arrived via agents, R.E. Trem Ltd of Finningley, who reclaimed and refurbished the actual diesel engines for further use. *Photo: Ken Fairey*

BELOW: Sixteen years later, Southern Region 4-SUB units 4673 and 4682 stand in the same yard waiting for cutting to commence. *Photo: Colin Marsden*

TOP: Although most enthusiasts were aware of the large private yards that were in business during the heyday of steam and diesel disposals of the sixties, many were unaware of the existence of numerous small, often family concerns that were to be found throughout the country. One such small yard was Willoughby's at Choppington, Northumberland. This yard dealt with only a handful of locally withdrawn locomotives, mainly steam, and a single electric locomotive, namely 26501 from Heaton.

This was one of a pair of pioneer electric locomotives built by the NER in 1904 to operate the short Newcastle Quayside branch, which had the unenviable distinction of a tunnel with a 180 degree bend in the middle, a nightmare to steam train crews as it trapped steam and smoke. When the north Tyneside loop was electrified at the turn of the century, the opportunity was taken to electrify the branch and so alleviate the problem. The two locomotives worked the branch until withdrawal in 1964. 26500 was claimed for the national collection, while 26501 passed to Willoughby's where it is seen on the 7th August 1966. Note the former NER livery which had been restored to both locomotives in 1961. *Photo I.S. Carr*

BOTTOM: It is a strange fact that although many steam engines were sold to Woodham's at Barry, only four diesels found their way to the most famous scrap yard of all. These were: two first series Warships D600 *Active* and D601 *Ark Royal*; BTH D8206; and NB D6122. The presence of D6122 at Barry was in itself curious. By the late sixties, all the class were allocated to depots in Scotland where they were giving numerous problems. Some were re-engined with Paxman-Ventura engines and reclassified Class 29. Others were in store, including D6122 at Inverurie Works. In November 1967 it was sent south to Hither Green for use in re-railing exercises. However, the following month found it withdrawn from service and languishing at Hither Green depot. There it was to remain until July 1968, when it was sent to Barry. Unlike the remainder of the class, which were quickly cut following withdrawal, D6122 remained at Barry until the summer of 1980 when it was finally cut for scrap. *Photo: Graham Scott-Lowe*

The role of the private yards

The role of BREL

By 1970, the mass withdrawals of the previous three years were coming to an end, albeit only temporarily. Only a few examples of non-standard classes remained in service and the private yards found their supplies of redundant locomotives dwindling. Those that remained operational had to look to new sources of railway material, diesel and electric multiple units, coaches and wagons.

On the Western Region, although reliability of the diesel-hydraulic classes was on a par with their diesel-electric counterparts, this was at a much greater maintenance cost, hence bringing into question the future of the hydraulics. Changes in railway traffic towards the end of the sixties meant that the re-organization of locomotive fleets would allow for the total withdrawal of all hydraulic classes by 1977. Mass withdrawals again commenced with no fewer than 106 hydraulic locomotives being taken out of traffic between October 1971 and January 1972. Unlike the sixties when withdrawn stock was sold off to private contractors, these latest withdrawals almost all ended their days at BREL Swindon. During the early seventies, long lines of redundant hydraulics awaiting cutting at Swindon were a common sight for travellers passing the works by rail. The west end of the works rapidly filled as more and more loco-motives arrived from depots throughout the Western Region.

In Scotland, BREL Glasgow was gradually cutting the ill fated Class 17 Claytons. Following the withdrawal of the hydraulics, further withdrawals during the seventies were limited to a few diesel shunters and accident damage victims. However, once again the lull was only temporary, as the Class 24s came to the end of their working lives and were dispatched to both Swindon and Doncaster. These were joined by early examples of Class 25. By the late seventies it appeared that no class was safe. 08s, 20s, 31s, 40s, 44s, 45s, 46 and 55s were all being withdrawn in large numbers. Swindon continued to handle the lion's share of the withdrawals with Doncaster, Crewe, Derby and Glasgow playing lesser roles.

Occasionally, locomotives sent to works for repair or assessment are actually with-drawn on works when repair is found to be uneconomic. Generally, however, most loco-motives disposed of on works arrived after withdrawal; not all would be complete, many parts having been removed at depots in order to keep the remainder of the fleet operational. On entering the works, any remaining diesel fuel in the fuel tanks is removed prior to the locomotive being stripped of all re-usable components. These may not only be re-used on members of the same class, but also on different classes; a number of Class 37s, for example, are running on Class 55 bogies, and 37006 is fitted with a Class 40 nose cone. Once stripped of all useful components, the body shell has then to be cut, the final stage of disposal.

The time that withdrawn stock remains at BREL premises before finally being cut varies enormously between the different works and different classes, from a few days to several years.

For BREL, disposing of redundant life-expired stock is not the glamorous side of their operations. No gleaming new, high techno-logical end product to display for the media, just several truck loads of scrap metal to be quietly removed without fuss or ceremony.

ABOVE: The numbers of locos awaiting cutting at BREL works varies from works to works, and from year to year, and also depends on the amount of space available within the works for storage of redundant stock. Historically, several times during its history, Swindon has become a dumping ground for numerous withdrawn locomotives, both at the end of the broad gauge era and at the end of WR steam, then later at the end of the short lived hydraulic era and again as a result of the 1980 recession.

This view of Swindon in January 1977 shows just 10 of the 28 Westerns awaiting cutting on the works. Also present at Swindon on this date were eight class 24s and two 08 shunters, both of which can be seen. A feature of the Westerns in their final years was the display of their number within the, by now defunct, headcode panel, as shown by 1072 in the centre of this line-up.
Photo: Graham Scott-Lowe

The role of BREL

Horwich Works in Lancashire is reported only to have cut one diesel locomotive, namely 12001 (formerly LMS 7076 of 1936) back in 1962. However, many units were cut at Horwich, particularly from the Southern Region. Many miles from its home base of Wimbledon, 4-SUB 4648 awaits entry to the works on 3rd October 1981.
Photo: Colin Marsden

Unlike Swindon or Doncaster, Crewe has never cut large numbers of locomotives. However, when the 40s came to the end of their working days, many were sent to Crewe for removal of essential spares and the remaining body shell was then cut at the works.

Many 40s were stored at Flag Lane and Eagle Bridge, near to the electric depot. In this view from Eagle Bridge on 22nd March 1986, eight of the class can be seen waiting entry to The Melt Shop (out of picture on the left) for cutting. The Melt Shop was first used in a major diesel cutting role with the arrival in 1971 of the Class 15s from Ipswich, when 25 were cut at Crewe between November 1971 and April 1972. In the left background is the old cutting area where a number of diesels and electrics were cut in the sixties and seventies.
Photo: Keith Long

ABOVE: Withdrawals of WCML electric classes have gradually increased during the last years, with virtually all members of Classes 82, 83 & 84 now out of service. Even Classes 81 & 85 are not immune and their numbers will most certainly decrease over the coming months and years as new classes are introduced.

Crewe Works on 25th September 1985 and 81001, the pioneer E3001 first introduced in November 1959, awaits cutting. It was withdrawn in 1984 after catching fire while hauling a northbound Motorail service near Carstairs. Behind is 84008, which was withdrawn in October 1979. It was still there at the end of 1986 and must be in line to be one of the locomotives remaining extant longest after withdrawal. *Photo: Colin Marsden*

LEFT: The cab of 33043 was removed from the locomotive after it had been involved in an accident at Mottingham with 33036 on 11th October 1977, and was either awaiting repair for possible further use on another crash damage victim or was awaiting final cutting when photographed in August 1978. Although damaged in the accident, 33043 was not condemned. 33036 was less fortunate and had to be withdrawn after it had rolled down the embankment coming to rest in the back garden of 413 Sidcup Road! *Photo: Ian Cowley*

LEFT: The Peaks have become synonymous with the Midland during their working lives. 44002 (D2) was built at Derby in 1959 and scrapped there 20 years later, having spent most of those 20 years working freight turns out of Toton. When photographed on 1st September 1979, cutting had been limited to the removal of the number panels for selling off to enthusiasts. Complete cutting took place over the following two months.
Photo: Ian Cowley

The role of BREL

RIGHT: Views at Swindon of locomotives awaiting scrapping are almost always outside. In fact, although final cutting usually takes place outside at Swindon, stripping of components is an inside job, where expensive parts are protected from adverse weather conditions.

Class 40 40127 is seen being stripped on 16th June 1983, some 16 months after withdrawal. Class 40 cylinder heads are vital components to be salvaged for re-use in other English Electric machines, namely Classes 20 & 37. At 1986 prices, cylinder heads were valued at £1000 each, and with a Class 40 possessing 16 cylinders, their removal was prudent. It is also this need to recover cylinder heads that could limit BR sales of any further Class 40s to preservation societies at basic scrap value.
Photo: John Stretton

The role of BREL

LEFT: On a grey, misty winter's day, the sparks fly as the cutter gets his oxy-acetylene torch to work on the metal work around the cab door of 24109. The locomotive had arrived at the works a few weeks earlier after being in store, with many others of the class, for more than two years at Kingmoor Yard, Carlisle. This particular engine was one of a batch of ten fitted with air compressors, and allocated when new to Gateshead depot for use on the Tyne Dock–Consett iron-ore trains. *Photo: John Chalcraft*

BELOW: A shroud of snow silently covers the remains of 40003 in the cutting area at Doncaster on 22nd January 1984. Note the wagons behind 40003 into which the scrap is loaded as cutting proceeds. The scrapping of the 40s at Doncaster followed a set pattern; after the removal of the roof, bodyside and nose cone panels, the power unit and subsidiary components were recovered. Finally the cabs were taken off, leaving the chassis for final cutting. *Photo: R.S.M. Brown*

LEFT: Changes in freight patterns and the associated closure of yards and depots has resulted in British Rail's once extensive fleet of larger 0-6-0 shunters being dramatically reduced over the years; from the withdrawal of the early pre-nationalisation classes, through the non-standard Lister-Blackstone examples, to the mass withdrawals in recent years of the highly successful Class 08s. During the past six years, Swindon and Doncaster have between them cut most of the withdrawn 08s. It is at the latter works, in July 1984, that the remains of 08381 await final cutting. It had entered service some 27 years earlier at Hither Green, originally numbered D3466.
Photo: Keith Long

BELOW: Cutting of 40047 is well advanced at Doncaster on 15th December 1985. Note the metal skips in the foreground for various components recovered during scrapping.
Photo: Richard Lillie

The vast majority of the Class 25s have been cut at Swindon. Only towards the end of their working days were a number sent to Doncaster. 25302 is seen here being cut in June 1986. The Class 25s were some of the last locomotives to be cut at Doncaster before the major reorganisation of BREL in 1986-87. In fact, a lack of space in the autumn of 1986 meant that the final batches of locomotives sent to Doncaster for scrapping were resold to Berry's at Leicester. *Photo: Richard Lillie*

The role of BREL

ABOVE: Cutting conditions at Crewe are, in comparison with most BREL Works, good, being totally undercover in the former Melts shop. This is an area of the works eagerly anticipated by parties of visiting enthusiasts, as it is here that one can see the remains of locomotives recently cut and being cut. Number panels cut from the cab side are often to be found laying around, a clue to the previous few weeks' work.

On 25th September 1985, a stream of sparks from between the bogies of 40024 show that the cutters are at work inside the body shell. This particular loco was a firm favourite with railtour operators and it had been hoped that it might be preserved. *Photo: Colin Marsden*

RIGHT: The Scottish Region has remained very much an individual, retaining specific classes and individual locomotives. Until 1987, Scotland had to be visited to see Classes 26 and 27 in any numbers, for it is here that they have made their home over the last 25 years. Both classes have proved reliable and recently the 26s have been the subject of heavy overhaul and refurbishment designed to prolong their lives. Only in recent times have in-roads been made into the 27s but in 1987 mass withdrawals of the class took place and by August, all had gone. Just prior to this, Glasgow Works ceased to be part of BREL and cutting at the works ended. As a result, large numbers of the Class 27s were sold to Berry's and began the long journey south for cutting.

Glasgow will be remembered as the final resting place for early withdrawn 27s many of which were fire victims, 27031 being an example. It was cut at Glasgow Works during September 1978 and when photograaphed the following month, only the cabs remained. *Photo: Steve Turner*

The present day

It is now over 30 years since the 1955 Modernisation Plan was conceived and implemented. Many classes of diesels announced at that time have long since passed into obscurity and new classes have arrived to take their place. There have been years that have seen large numbers of locomotives withdrawn: the late sixties — a time of closures, and the early seventies — the end of the hydraulics. After a comparative lull, the early eighties saw recession hit BR freight traffic and large scale withdrawals followed due to a surplus of motive power. Now, in the second half of the eighties, withdrawals continue at a steady rate. Classes 25 and 27 were rendered extinct in 1987 whilst the numbers of Class 45s continue to fall steadily. Meanwhile, inroads began into both Classes 33 and 47.

Clearly, financial limits restrict spending on new types. A programme of major refurbishment of classes 26 and 47 is complete and now the class 37s are passing through BREL Crewe for a rebuild which will see what is arguably one of the most successful classes remaining in service through to the twenty-first century. At present, the locomotive operating fleet is at an optimum number and a further major reduction seems unlikely without a new build programme providing alternative motive power. However, as was seen during the recession, a change in economic fortunes of the country as a whole, could easily have major repercussions for BR.

Over the past 15 years, the great majority of locomotives withdrawn by BR had ended their days at Swindon, with a much lower percentage being disposed of at Crewe, Doncaster, Derby and Glasgow. The closure of Swindon in the spring of 1986 left about 100 locos remaining on the works awaiting cutting. Throughout the summer of 1986, this number dwindled steadily as cutting proceeded. By September, Berry's of Leicester had become involved with disposals at Swindon, part cutting locos at the works, and transporting complete cabs back to their yard for final breaking. The remaining diesel bodies were being cut for scrap at Swindon and sent to South Wales for export.

Cutting of locos at Derby had all but ceased during 1986 and Crewe had undertaken only limited scrapping, in the form of Class 47s, during the year. Doncaster continued to cut until the autumn of 1986 but at a rate much reduced to that planned, their schedule being many months behind target. When the former DMU shop at Doncaster was closed in September 1986, to be converted into a central stores, a lack of space within the works meant locos awaiting disposal had to be towed back out of the works and were put to store at Goole, only to be sold to Berry's in the autumn of 1986.

The Southern Region is at present disposing of its own stock on site. Several class 33s were withdrawn at the beginning of 1986 to supply essential spares to keep the remainder of the fleet operational. When these had been stripped at Eastleigh depot, the remains were cut on site by BR staff.

Several LMR withdrawals were also dealt with on site during 1986, again, by Berry's. Meanwhile, in Scotland, a considerable number of withdrawn 08 shunters were sold off to private dealers — the first private disposal sale north of the border for many years. During 1987, large numbers of redundant Class 27s built up throughout Scotland awaiting disposal; the presence of asbestos within this class causing disposal problems. Former Eastfield locomotive 27043, which for many years lay at the back of the depot being used for rerailing exercises had already been 'lost' by cocooning it in polythene and dumping it in the bottom of a rubbish tip at Mount Vernon, Glasgow. The remainder of the class were sold to Berry's at Leicester and a steady stream of locomotives were towed south to Leicester throughout the summer of 1987.

Although diesel withdrawals may be currently passing through a relatively slack period, on the multiple unit front the complete opposite is true. During the seventies, as with diesel locomotives, a refurbishment plan was implemented in order to extend the life of a number of units until a second generation could be introduced to traffic. The refurbished units should remain in service for some time yet but as BR now introduces into service its second generation of DMUs, and as new electrification schemes come on line, so the older units are rapidly being phased out. Many of these contain the deadly blue asbestos which, regulations dictate, needs to be removed by specialist firms. Two such firms, Berry's of Leicester and Mayer Newmans of Snailwell, Newmarket, have between them handled virtually all BR unit withdrawals over the past 10 years. With vehicles containing asbestos due to be phased out by early 1989, and with more new units coming into service each month, withdrawals must continue at their present rate for many months.

ABOVE: For Class 47 devotees, 1987 will be remembered as the year withdrawals commenced in earnest. With major repairs not now being carried out on the older examples fitted with series parallel traction motors these, and life expired members of the class, are being withdrawn to provide a reserve of spare parts for cost effective maintenance. Although some are providing spares at depots, BREL Crewe has the job of reclaiming reusable components from most withdrawn members. Once stripped, the bodies are being cut in the old Melts shop. Smoke rises from the cab of 47529 as the cutter removes a cabside panel on 9th April 1987. 47152 behind, met the same fate a few days later. *Photo: Brian Morrison*

RIGHT: July 30th 1984 saw a major railway disaster in Scotland when a Glasgow-Edinburgh push-pull train, headed by DBSO 9706 and propelled by 47707 *Holyrood*, hit a cow which had strayed onto the line at Polmont. Several coaches received serious damage and were later cut at Greenhill Upper Junction. On 19th November, work is well advanced on cutting TSO 12006. Following this accident, all push-pull DBSOs were modified and fitted with small 'cow-catchers' in order to minimise the possibility of similar accidents. *Photo: Colin Marsden*

BELOW: At the beginning of 1986, many withdrawn Scottish 08 shunters were sold to Glasgow scrap merchants J.R. Adams and J. McWilliams. On February 13th a long line awaits processing at Adam's yard, London Road. Headed by 09346 the row contains: 08341, 08175, 08227, 08196, 08347, 08424, 08321, 08319, 08326, 08312, plus one unidentifiable example. Some of these had been withdrawn for a number of years, the longest serving being 08175, withdrawn from Grangemouth in December 1978. *Photo: Tom Noble*

LEFT, TOP: When British Rail withdrew large numbers of diesel shunters in the late sixties, many were almost new and hardly run-in. At this time, BR was selling redundant stock by tender and, although many went for scrap, large numbers were purchased for re-use by industrial concerns. Some, like British Steel, ran large fleets of ex-BR locomotives, while others were to obtain just a single example. Even now, some 15-20 years later, a considerable number of these locomotives remain in service. Others have been withdrawn for a second time; sometimes for mechanical reasons, others because their colliery or similar work place has closed down. Of all the industrial users, the National Coal Board (now British Coal), ran the largest fleet of ex-BR locomotives. The Philadelphia workshops near Sunderland, Tyne and Wear, closed on the 19th July 1985. By November 10th 1985 work was well advanced on cutting 509. Formerly Class 11 12119, it had arrived at Philadelphia in February 1969 and had spent the next 16 years working in the coal fields around Sunderland. Behind 509 are partially dismantled 512 (12060) and 514 (12084). *Photo: Ian Carr*

LEFT, BOTTOM: Although most withdrawn locos are disposed of at BREL works or sold to private contractors, a number have been cut on depots, once stripped of all reusable components. With more repairs taking place at Level 5 depots, such occurrences may well become more common.

One of the first depots where a locomotive was cut up on site was Old Oak Common. Class 31 31254 was withdrawn from Immingham on December 1st 1979. Later in the month, it was towed to Old Oak Common TMD where it provided spares for the fleet of 31s that Old Oak were running at the time. After stripping, the body shell was cut in the first few months of 1980. Only one cab and a few parts were left when photographed on 4th March 1980; by July, even these had disappeared. With the exception of the original pilot scheme examples, only a handful of these Brush built Class 31s have been withdrawn. *Photo: Colin Marsden*

THIS PAGE: In the heart of the Cambridge-shire countryside, just a few miles north west of Newmarket, lies the small picturesque village of Snailwell. On the outskirts of the village, hidden by a line of trees and adjacent to the Newmarket-Ely line, is Mayer Newman's extensive and highly efficient scrap yard. During the past few years, many hundreds of units and coaches have reached the end of their working lives in this yard.

All coaching stock contains a high proportion of combustible material, from seats to internal wooden body panels. Whilst most small yards set fire to coaches prior to cutting, a not particularly efficient operation, at Snailwell, Mayer Newman's operate a very large incinerator which completes the job in a matter of minutes, leaving only a tangled burnt out metallic shell to be cut.

One such victim is an unidentified Park Royal dmu photographed on 27th June 1984. It will not be many hours before it too joins the pile of scrap metal visible in the foreground. *Photo: Ian Cowley*

The present day

A scrapyard in close-up:
Berry's scrapyard, Leicester

One yard that has handled BR withdrawals for a number of years is Berry's at Leicester. From the first sales of a few coaches, Berry's has become one of the most important outlets of BR redundant stock and with a declining role for BREL, Berry's have expanded rapidly in this field.

Their Leicester yard is situated on the site of the former Great Central goods yard to the east of the old Great Central main line. A rail link to the Midland main line allows easy access of stock in, and scrap out of the yard. The yard has attracted increasing interest from enthusiasts over the past years. Upperton Road overbridge, which spans much of the yard, gives outstanding views of stock being dealt with, reminiscent of Cashmore's famous steam-breaking yard at Newport.

There is always considerable activity in Berry's and plenty to see. As many as 20 withdrawn units can be dealt with in a month, and a team of men is able to cut a locomotive in a day. To assist in moving stock around within the yard once it has been tripped in by BR, Berry's run a former 03 shunter, 03069. Leicester must be the only location in the country where one can view both diesel and electric multiple units from the Southern, Eastern, London Midland and Scottish regions.

One of the assets of Berry's is its asbestos removal facilities. Safe removal of blue asbestos is a requisite prior to final cutting of the remaining body shell. Berry's are not only involved with scrapping, their asbestos removal facility is used by BR for non-withdrawn stock. During 1987, a number of diesel multiple-units have visited the yard to have asbestos removed. The following photographs graphically portray the various processes involved in reducing once resplendent locomotives and multiple units to manageable piles of scrap metal.

The famous locomotive stack at Berry's is not the first to have been built at the yard, as this 22nd August 1986 view of Class 120 units shows. *Photo: Paul Biggs*